CAMPING

LECTOR HOUSE PUBLIC DOMAIN WORKS

CAMPING

ALEXANDRA AGUSTA GUTTMAN LOCKWINE
(BIDDY)

9 789356 145979
ISBN: 978-93-5614-597-9

Published: -

LECTOR HOUSE

LECTOR HOUSE LLP
E-MAIL: info@lectorhouse.com

CAMPING

BY

BIDDY

Known in Real Life as

ALEXANDRA AGUSTA G. LOCKWINE, R. N.

ILLUSTRATED

DEDICATION

To Dr. George Alexander Kohut, who may not be a good judge of whiskey, but who is a Gentleman and a Scholar, one of the few Preachers who does as he says, this book is affectionately dedicated by the author.

February 14, 1911

FOREWORD

NOWADAYS, whenever we pick up a magazine, we read the notices of Camps all the way from Maine to California, who are in need of Campers, and think how very popular camping is becoming, when as a matter of fact it is the one and only pastime that has always retained its popularity.

We can trace it back to the prehistoric ages; see it carved in hieroglyphics on obelisks, find upon investigation that North, South, East or West, the tribes of Red, Black, Yellow and White, have gloried in living in tents, so is it any wonder that mankind still loves it?

This thin veneer of civilization which makes us desire to shut ourself in structures of brick and wood is only skin deep. Right under the surface the love for the open prevails so strongly, that every little while a man who has been brought up according to our standards breaks loose, takes to the road and lives a life of freedom, while the world looking on pities him for going down in the scale and tries to bring him back from the life his nature craves, to one of humdrum existence.

Then come along with me, please, do, for just one summer in Camp and you will say at the end of the season that you can squeeze more fun into a canvas tent than into all the palaces you ever were in.

CONTENTS

CAMPING

CHAPTER I.

GETTING READY.

With the catalog and prospectus in front of you, making delightful little shivers run up and down your spine, you begin marking down, first, the articles you must have; then the things you hope your fond relatives will give you; then the clothes and athletic goods without which any boy with true camping spirit cannot get along.

Your father, who secretly expects to come out to Camp and use some of your cherished sweaters, running pants, swimming trunks, etc., etc., suggests that you get extra large sizes, to allow for shrinkage. You protest, telling him that you don't want your clothes to look like "hand-me-downs," that you had inherited from your big brother.

After many heart-breaking wrenches, during which you feel as though even death itself were preferable to giving up all the articles you have chosen, you effect a compromise by saying you will be satisfied with one fishing rod, six pairs of running pants, several pairs of sneakers, lots of sweaters, a complete outfit of oilskins, tennis racket, baseball bat, balls, and Oh! what a good boy you would be, if you could have a canoe.

You would study all winter, not want to stay up late, cross your heart to leave cigarettes and trashy novels alone, but, gee whiz! only to be the owner of a canoe. You even appeal to your father, who weighs in the neighborhood of 200 pounds, and try to make him see the fun of going out with you. Suppose you were upset? What of it? You can both swim.

Mother, dear, puts a quick veto on that. No canoe for you at any price. In fact, owing to her nervous system being in need of recuperation, she thinks the bath tub the best place to swim in, and deplores the risks one must take in order to be athletic.

The 'House' having vetoed the canoe question, you offer another little bill, asking for an appropriation for a shotgun, or at least one of those dandy little air rifles, so you can shoot at targets and the farmers' cows and chickens.

Before you can be heard the 'House' vetoes that, too. Danger signals are displayed, and you feel as though you were treading on a third rail.

The 'House' suggests that you should spend the summer with her, taking views with your Kodak, walking miles every day and playing ping pong and lotto every evening, thus getting a nice quiet rest to prepare you for a long winter's study.

In the deepest despair you clutch your father's hand. He gives you a sympathetic squeeze in return. Say, is there anything on the face of this earth like the loving freemasonry between a sporty parent and his little son?

Not to agitate matters any more and change the subject, you ask how much pocket money you are to be allowed per week. The 'House' again rises to object, claiming that, as there are no car fares to be paid or soda fountains to tempt, you cannot have any possible use for money. You will be furnished with plenty of paper and stamped envelopes and sundries, thus for once relieving you of the strain of handling money.

Well, whoever heard of a right little, tight little boy who objected to the jingle of loose change in his pants pockets? "If such there be, go mark him well," for he surely will need watching.

From data you have gathered, you inform the 'House' that a camel with three stomachs isn't in it with a hungry boy at Camp; that your special friends, Jack, Ed, and Fatty, all spend their weekly money, and that nothing but the fear of being punished keeps them from gnawing the canvas tents. They live in the open all the time and are constantly hungry.

Just about the time when one feels that hunger laughs at locksmiths, the ice cream and cake man drives in. If you have ever in your travels seen a horde of hungry little piglings swarm all over a trough you can form some idea of what those boys do to that wagon. The boys are simply starving for ice cream and cake. One plate is only an introduction; with the second one you begin to distinguish the flavor; it really needs a third one to put that sweet icy feeling in your stomach so earnestly desired by the growing youth. The next day, or maybe next but one, our friend the fruit man calls. All your life you have been told of the value of fruit. Your system at this time craves lots of it. It is very good for you. Oh! yes, certainly! but it has to be paid for from some of that pocket money. All this and more you tell them, being careful to cross your t's and dot your i's for fear of the 'House's' objections.

Father and mother decide to consult together. You see the moment has arrived, when you will gain more by saying less, so you kiss them good-night and "stand not upon the order of your going."

Upstairs you fall into a brown study. With your clothes half off, you think of the fun you will have; perhaps of the medals you will win, and there creeps just a little undercurrent of sadness through you at the thought of parting from your devoted parents. "Ah, me! I kind of hate to leave mother," you think, then console yourself that they will be coming up to see you. About this time your day dream ends suddenly, for they are coming upstairs. Out goes the light. Into bed you jump. Are asleep in the twinkling of an eye, to dream that you are at Camp, enjoying all the fun and frolic there.

The minute you open your eyes in the morning you read the catalog from beginning to end, look at the pictures, try to fancy yourself posing as the champion high diver, jumper and tennis player, and forget to brush your teeth, in your hurry to get to school, where you can consult with your chums.

Not one sporting goods window can you pass without a curious glance. In fact, dear boy, you are in such a maze that when the teacher asks you to tell him how you would start for the North Pole you answer promptly: "From the Grand Central Station, on the Bar Harbor Express," and, for the life of you, cannot see why the class roars at you.

Some weeks never seem to come to an end, and this, the very longest week of your life, just crawls away. Saturday your fond father has promised to go with you and purchase the athletic goods, while mother attends to the rest.

You want to know where he is going to buy them and what he is going to get. Are told to come along and not fuss any more. If there is any smell on the face of this earth that smells nicer than new leather in an athletic goods shop, I want to smell it. Oh, me! Oh, my! what beauties, and you have to bite your tongue to keep from interrupting.

Business has been very good with father, and he, thinking back over his own boyhood, when money was as scarce as hens' teeth, makes up his mind to fit you out so as to be a credit to yourself and him.

Later in life you may blossom out in a Prince Albert and silk hat, a dinner or full dress suit, but never, as long as you live, will clothes ever give you the unalloyed pleasure that these camping togs do in your first year at Camp.

As a rule, you are not over and above fond of carrying bundles. The cook can vouch for that. How much bribery she had to practice to make you bring home quickly a bottle of milk or of water or a bunch of soup greens. But now you are perfectly willing to carry everything from sneakers to caps, and can hardly trust the salesman to send them home.

In the privacy of your room you strip off your clothes in a jiffy, for the joy of trying on the different sweaters, running pants and swimming trunks. In your baseball clothes you pose, in fancy, almost a miniature Mathewson; try a high dive from the bureau to the bed; do a hurdle over the towel rack. Nothing but the fear of breaking the furniture stops you in your wild gambols.

Another peep at the catalog to see if you have everything you need; a fervent hope that you may make good, and bring home with you in the fall a silver cup or trophy. Then, carefully folding each and every garment with almost reverent care, you vow to keep your trunk in order. If any one should mention the fact to you, you would be indignant at the idea of not caring a jot at the end of the season whether you collected your belongings or left them lying around loose.

Among the gifts you have thus far received are a compass, a kodak and a housewife filled with thread, needles, buttons, etc. There does not seem to be one thing wanting to make life one long, sweet song unless it is the canoe which you hope for next year. All through life that one little thing which would make us perfectly happy, if we had it, and yet the perfect happiness is not for mortals. Truly, the poet knew what he was talking about when he said,

> "Not enjoyment, and not sorrow,
> Is our destined end or way;
> But to act, that each to-morrow
> Find us farther than to-day."

CHAPTER II.

LEAVING THE CITY.

A few days before we leave for Camp all the boys, new and old, are invited to meet at the home of the Director to become acquainted with one another. It is called a rally, and truly the boys do rally around the Director, whose greatest fault is that he loves mankind too much, for his idea of Heaven is that it is filled with boys alone. One look in his face will convince the most skeptical, and association for even a brief season with him makes a boy feel truer and better.

The principal part of the rally consists of partaking bountifully of ice cream, cake and lemonade, while exchanging yarns with old friends, making new acquaintances, thinking up new jokes, and enjoying the shining hours. The faculty hobnob with each other, and, taking it altogether, it is a delightful afternoon, one to be remembered as a red letter day.

Even the old Camp nurse calls around, to be greeted by both her friends and enemies; to renew her friendship for all, mentally picking out new favorites, while keeping a warm spot in her heart for old boys. There is something in the air that starts her off right away using camp slanguage, and behaving like one of the boys. She just cannot help getting into the spirit of the thing. All the way over to the rally she had told herself that she must act in a dignified way becoming to a woman of 80 in the shade, then the minute she catches sight of the crowd she throws dignity to the winds, saying she'll none of it, is ready for a tussle with or without gloves, snaps her fingers at old Father Time. Let the sands run down if they must, but until the last grain has run, she hopes to be with her boys, to tease, to love, to try and care for them. If they need a mother's care, all right; she is there. Are they in want of a chum? Well, in a pinch she will do. As long as she can make them happy in her poor little way, what cares she if she does make a goose of herself?

You see that, after all, the keynote of life is LOVE. With it, the very poorest home is happy; without it, a palace is dreary. So poor old Nursie starts out by loving the Director, and right on down the line, finding good qualities in the worst and tamest boy there. She is devoutly thankful for the chance to spend some weeks with those who love her, despite her years and looks.

But we must not get mushy. So let's travel along and get to the starting point, or how shall we ever get there?

The day before we leave New York the expressman calls for our trunks, bags, etc., which ends our troubles as far as they are concerned. We never see anything of them until we get to Camp, yet they have been on their way just the same as we.

There they stand on the Campus, waiting to be put into the tents. They are filled with good things to decorate and make these little homes look like college rooms.

The long-looked-for day is here at last. A farewell look around to see that we have forgotten nothing, we make a solemn promise to write regularly, to keep our teeth clean, not to eat much trash, to keep out of danger, not to get wet, to mind the Director and faculty; in fact, to be good, good, good.

Compared to the excitement at the depot, the Tower of Babel was a peaceful village. Of course, it is a fool comparison to compare the anxious parents' wanderings to that of a lot of hens who have just been decapitated, yet they will feel so terribly anxious at the parting moment. Every mother wants her boy looked after, never mind the rest. The boy himself doesn't want to be fussed over, and most awfully hates to be petted in public.

Yes, sir! I have known boys who would kick at being petted in public, and yet were perfectly willing to have some one lie down with them at night, telling them fairy stories until they were sleepy. They never entirely get over that, either, only the tables are reversed in later years, they being the ones to tell the fairy stories.

The gates are opened; one wild rush for the cars; mothers kissing the wrong boys in their excitement; everybody trying to get away from somebody else, the inevitable small boy with fiendish cunning letting go of your hand, shouts, laughter, tears and prayers, follow us as we step aboard the special train reserved for our Camp, "Good-bye, dear—Be a good boy—Write soon—Clean your teeth—Don't poke your head out of the window—Tell the Nurse about your medicine—Tell the faculty about your clothes—Ask the doctor to keep an eye on you—Let the Director 'phone me as soon as you get there"—these, and a thousand and one more questions and orders, follow us as we slowly glide out of the train shed.

We soothe the nervous parents, honestly promising them to look after their darlings, send them home with sometimes a heavy heart at the thought of parting from their children, yet thankful that they can give them advantages that they themselves could not always have in their youth. There are, of course, exceptions; many a father realizes that he has not the knack of training his boys and being wise, decides to let others do it for him. For what on earth is sadder than parent and child who do not understand each other, constantly pulling at the wrong end of the rope, growing farther and farther apart as the years go by.

Before the train is in the tunnel the little chaps are peeling off their collars, ties and all the clothes they dare, having been almost roasted, that hot June evening, before starting.

The porter is ordered to make up berths at once. You really would think they wanted to go to bed. It looks that way for a minute, but is only a huge bluff. While ample room has been allowed for all, the rascals prefer getting into each other's berths. Only the very little boys go to sleep before 10 or 11 p. m. Such a glorious time as they have! But even the wildest boy must let up some time until his storage batteries are recharged. At last quiet prevails, and for the next few hours nothing is heard but the click of the rails, the warning whistle, the brakeman passing through the cars with shining lantern, one or another of the faculty seeing that all's well, our Director himself looking out for the comfort of the little ones.

Biddy herself, on the job, like the old woman of nursery rhyme who had so many children she didn't know what to do, is put down at one end of the car with all the littlest ones. These she can watch (when she's awake), and gather under her wings in case of storm. There is no storm, unless one of protest at the general racket made.

CHAPTER III.

ON THE WAY TO CAMP.

The night passes at last. With the first streak of daylight boys jump up and dress quickly, for we are due at Portland a little after 7 a. m.

Our breakfast has been ordered ahead. All we have to do is to eat it, not like the famous recipe for cooking a hare; ours has been caught, skinned and cooked. It seems to fill the bill, for with good appetite we fall to, causing even the waiters, who are used to almost everything, to gasp at the way the food disappears.

About half an hour is allowed us at the station. Then "All aboard" for Oxford. What a beautiful country we are passing through! The late spring here makes everything look beautifully tender and green; rolling country, which, after all, is the perfect landscape, passes before us. After the heat and dust of the city, how cool and refreshing this is! Comfortable farm houses, lovely orchards, with the trees heavy with young fruit, winding streams, songbirds on every side, overhead a sky of tenderest blue, with here and there a fleck of white—even the cattle grazing in the fields seem to know that we are coming, for they low, and the calves run along the inside of the fence seeming to recognize kindred spirits. Through this most beautiful section of country we ride for one and one-half hours, stopping at Oxford.

Carriages are waiting for the 6-mile ride to Camp. We thought Nature in her most lavish mood had shown us the best she had while we were on the train, but here were more and more surprises in store for us. Were you to take a little of Lake George, mix it with some shady lanes in England, add the clear atmosphere of the Catskills, sprinkle around a few of the prettiest lakes in Switzerland, borrow the Italian skies for a covering, even then, Maine, in this section, can give the rest of the country cards and spades and beat them at that.

We are really very glad, though, when we come in sight of Camp. Even the loveliest drive won't satisfy a boy who is anxious to get to his tent. He wants to get out of his city clothes, and into Camp attire. What a beautiful scene opens before us! The lake, like a sheet of polished silver, rows of tents waiting for tenants, the tables already set for dinner, all the house help on hand smiling a welcome, and willing to make every one feel quickly at home.

Wagon after wagon drives up and discharges its load of living freight. They climb out any way, over the back, over the dashboard, over the wheels, the farmers threatening to sue for damages for injuries inflicted upon their ancient turnouts.

CHAPTER IV.

FIRST DAY IN CAMP.

Before we can locate ourselves the bugle sounds for mess. Each of the instructors has a certain number of boys in his care, so there is not the slightest confusion.

There is not a roof garden or a palm room or any other make-believe place for eating outdoors in the city that can compare with this. To eat out-of-doors with such air, such views, such food! Those who are hungry pitch right in; those with little appetite begin to eat, gaining a love for the food as they go along. Second helpings of everything are called for and eaten, until at last the waistband protests at such pressure being put upon it.

As soon as the signal is given to leave the table every boy takes quick advantage of it. We see them, running here and there, looking for their bags and boxes. For the next few hours they are as busy as the proverbial bee.

Boys, who, when at home, have not even as much as taken their changes of linen out of the bureau, who since infancy have been washed, combed, brushed and dressed by fond mothers and nurses, here learn for the first time what it is to do for themselves.

It is a joyful revelation to them to find out how much they can do. Heretofore they have not only been willing to let others do for them but have demanded it; now, when they need a bath, there is no one to prepare it for them, so they just go ahead and gather their belongings together and run down to the lake. No shutting of windows and taking a bath in a torrid temperature, with some one handy to rub your back, following that with an alcohol rub. I guess not. You go into water that sparkles, slop around if you cannot swim; swim around if you cannot slop. The water just soaks out all the impurities. Then out you jump. Sometimes you dry with a towel, most of the time the sun dries you, and of all the lovely towels on the face of this earth the pleasant sunshine, woven with gentle breezes, is the one and only towel for me.

In the city a chap just hurries into the water, soaps the washrag, debates, if he is in a hurry, whether to wash from head to foot or just touch the dirty places lightly and depend upon the towel to do the rest. Sometimes he sits down in the tub and doesn't wash at all; just sits there, thinking, like a bump on a log, until he is warned of the flight of time; then jumps out again, not half clean.

But at Camp the joy of going into the water is doubled, nay, trebled, by the knowledge that you cannot go in when you want to, but must wait until the proper hour; and this, our first day there, is about the middle of the afternoon.

Most of us fancy we can swim well until we go into a large body of water. There is all the difference in the world between making a fast sprint in a tank, under cover, with no currents or wind or shoaling water to impede one's movements. That is why so many boys have to find out for themselves the difference. Many boys who have held records for indoor swimming make rather poor showing when it comes to long-distance swimming in the open.

Our first afternoon at Camp passes so quickly that before you can say Jack Robinson it is time for supper. We have not done one-quarter of the self-imposed tasks. How can a fellow do much when he just has to stop every few seconds to look out of his tent? The water allures with its sparkle, the woods invite you to come and rest in their shade; the Campus begs for your company; baseball diamonds plead for just one game; tennis courts spread their nets to catch the player; basketball courts coax with their goals on high; the running track dares you to sprint just once around. What, with flags floating, sun shining, life and animation everywhere, is it any wonder that supper time finds us this day with happiness in our hearts, trunks upset, tents half decorated, letters to parents begun, everything started and nothing finished? On this, our first day, there is not one boy in a hundred who could put his share of the tent in order.

Take, for instance, the Kodak fiend. How can he bother with such things as arranging his toilet articles, when the sun is just right for snapping a few views? He surely can put his share in order when the shadows begin to fall. He uses up a roll of films without much result, because in his hurry to snapshot the entire country in one afternoon he makes mistakes. Later on he will discriminate, to his advantage, and by the end of the season show some pictures worth while.

Then there is the boy who has brought his musical instrument along to Camp. No matter whether it is a mandolin or a guitar, a violin or a drum, a banjo or jewsharp, it is an instrument, isn't it? sometimes of pleasure, most of the time of torture to the sensitive nerves, still with the best of intentions he tightens the keys, looks up at the ridge pole for inspiration and lets her go. He may play some selection from Beethoven or Chopin in a way to touch one's heart, causing work to cease while he plays. Then again it may be ragtime played out of time and tune, making one's fingers itch to slap him and destroy his musical instrument; but, no matter what it is, it is done for pleasure, and is accepted as such by his admiring tentmates.

So much for art and music. Then there is the boy who is anxious to start a game. That chap is to be really pitied. No matter how many times he puts the bat in the corner of his tent it has a sneaking way of rolling back again to his feet. Could it speak, it would probably, in a wooden sort of voice, ask what he had brought it along for. No bat with a bit of self-respecting feeling in its wooden heart likes to look new. It feels that its chief charm is to be useful more than ornamental, and if you are at all doubtful about the sympathetic feeling between a baseball bat and a good player, then just go to any one of the good games and watch the batters. Many a time have I been amused at their antics. They take up an apparently respectable old bat, swing it around, feel its weight, hit the ground with it, and just when you think that the bat in self-defense will swat them one they throw it down in disgust. The bat often rolls back again, asking for another trial. Has it not been created for just this kind of work? Then what right has a man to throw it down without a trial?

To an outsider there seems to be madness in their methods. Yet it may be the reverse, just as some people are created for one special line of work, so may even a piece of wood be better fitted to form a plank that stays in one place, while another piece of wood has so much life in it, whether you will or not, if you use that particular bat you are bound to win.

But for all-round madness, commend me to the tennis player. He is hopeless from the start, and all he knows about love is what he wins in the game. They will go without meals, play at all hours, and are as greedy as can be about holding on to courts. Yet tennis could be made a sentimental game. What with its couples, playing for love and courts, and nets, Cupid himself might take a hand in arranging the matches.

Well, the tennis fiend goes out, whether it is hot or cold, that first afternoon, finds a partner, runs, jumps and leaps all afternoon after two little white balls, with never a care as to whether his share of the tent is in order or not.

That is baseball and tennis for you, gentle reader.

Next, on this our first day, there is the boy who wants a boat and the boy who wants a swim.

No wonder poets have made verses about boating since time first was. Talk about the poetry of motion! To lie in the bottom of a roomy boat on a still lake on a sunny afternoon, the water lapping the sides in a gentle, soothing way, making us think of our mothers when they held us on their laps, just rocking so slowly and easily that we felt as if we cuddled up to her, her arms tight around us (as though to ward off all evil), and our head leaning on her breast, that heaven itself could offer nothing sweeter than this—indeed, if one had one's choice between being a little cherub a la Raphael, with cunning wings growing out of his shoulder blades, or just sitting on mother's lap and being loved, I rather think heaven would be short of cherubs, while every mother's lap would be filled.

Then why call a boy lazy who likes to lie idly in a boat, with his face turned up to the blue heavens? He probably is planning wonderful things to do when he grows up; in the meantime feeling an echo of the past, stirring his inmost being.

But of all the villains, the boy who wants a swim is the worst. He will do you the honor to ask for it, and is perfectly happy if you grant permission. He is evidently descended from some one of the original fishes who went into Noah's Ark. His nature craves water.

Long living on shore has rid his skin of any scaly look, but the fish blood is there just the same. He can dive to the bottom of the pool and stay there looking up at you with glassy eyes, for all the world like a sulky trout. When he leaps in the water you are reminded of a porpoise splashing through the foam at the vessel's bow. Again cutting through the water, half-submerged, how like a shark chasing its prey, this may consist of some harmless old female, who is gently ambling along. The first thing she knows some monster of the deep has grabbed her by the leg and is dragging her under water. She shrieks as in her struggles she fancies some dread sea monster is taking her to its lair. With almost superhuman effort she breaks loose, when the monster arises to laugh at her fright. It is the born swimmer, the descendant of prehistoric fishes, and the worst punishment you can give him is to keep him out of the water.

So much for the boatman and swimmer. By supper time most of the boys have laid the foundation for an elegant coat of tan, some will be badly sunburnt by to-morrow, for Old Sol dearly loves to scorch the tender skin of the city youth. It is useless to warn them about stripping all their clothes off too soon. How are they going to get a good coat of tan on by the end of the season if they don't begin right away? The only thing to do is to put plenty of oil on, and if "pain still treads on the heels of pleasure" they will learn the wisdom of making haste slowly.

We have a delightful supper. All of the boys do ample justice to it. Afterwards they lounge around for a short period, when again the bugle blows "Quarters."

Getting undressed in a tent with three other boys is lots of fun. There is no clothes closet to hang your clothes in, just a line made of rope or wire stretched across that serves as a clothes horse. The night is cool, and both front and back flaps of the tent are wide open to the breezes. Just half an hour is allowed to prepare for bed. Then the bugler sounds "Taps," the most beautiful call of all. Lights go out and silence reigns. Here and there laughter may be heard, but the majority of the boys are so tired that their heads have hardly touched the pillows before they are asleep, after one of the longest and happiest days of their lives.

CHAPTER V.

ROUTINE.

Bright and early the next morning the bugler sounds reveille. Every one jumps out of bed, although a few have already been up since daylight, so eager are they to be real Campers.

As soon as every one is out of bed the setting up exercises take place. For fifteen minutes the boys, under the leadership of the instructors, go through a course of calisthenics, after which they go down to the water for a scrub and plunge, brush their teeth and get their clothes on. By that time the bugle calls to them to get into line, ready to march to the table for breakfast.

All who are not on line-in will find themselves marching round the Campus, which is a block square, several times. Good exercise for them, at the same time teaching them the truth about "Time and tide waiting for no man."

Another good meal awaits us, plenty of good, substantial food, that will put strength into us and at the same time tickle our palate.

After breakfast we find that it is not all play at Camp. Some are inclined to loaf; some would like to wander around; others, with some definite object in view, plan to go out for practice runs or games. But, hold on, noble youths, you have slept in your beds, have you not? Well, like Mr. Squeers' method, we will ask you to spell "bed," then go and make it up. Also you have upset your tents. Again, you are given gracious permission to tidy them also.

Here we have no willing mothers, no handy chambermaids, to put everything in apple-pie order. This is truly Camp, and you are simply soldiers Camping.

The Director may have an orderly to do his work, but, as for the rest of the Campers, it is every man for himself, from the instructors down to the smallest boy. Each and every one must do his share. Beds are made, tents swept out, clothes hung up, and when the bugle again calls "Inspection" each and every boy must be at his tent.

The Director, accompanied by his staff, inspects, marking for and against each tent. Accordingly, there is keen competition between the boys to see who has the most orderly tent for the season. Prizes are awarded to the tent that has the best record. All this conduces to neat habits, and lets the boys see there is more to be gained by doing the right than the wrong thing.

Again the bugle calls for "Assembly." This is one of the most interesting events of the day. Here we can all sit under the shade of beautiful trees and listen to the orders being given out; the schedule of the games to be played; the list of those to be punished for breaking the rules, etc., etc. On this occasion the bad boy, knowing full well that he has been marked for punishment and is going to get it anyway, does a little more to amuse his friends while he annoys those in office.

As soon as the orders are given the boys are dismissed, some to go on the field for a game of tennis, others for baseball, others for walking trips. For the little boys there is tether ball and the junior baseball diamond. In fact, whatever is for the big boys is good for his little brothers, excepting football.

In the midst of the fun we hear the bugle again. That is the swimming call; so hurry with your bats, tennis rackets and any other thing you may be doing at this particular moment. Get your swimming trunks and rush down to the dock.

Now for fun. Those who can swim, how gracefully they dive in, swim under water, and just when your heart is in your mouth for fear they are drowned up they come in the opposite direction.

The boys who are not very good swimmers make up for skill by lots of splashing about in the shallow water. They duck each other, try to float, and act for all the world like a school of young porpoises. I myself like to go out with them. They take me for a friendly old mother whale and climb all over me, never so happy as when they get me down under the water. Then sometimes I take a large, roomy boat, invite them in and pole them around the lake to their enjoyment and my own, too.

But this chapter tells of routine, so we must obey the whistle when it blows. That means all out, and any one caught in after that is kept out for two or three times—about the worst kind of punishment you could give a boy.

Fortunately, the boys have very little dressing to do, a pair of running pants and a pair of sneakers being considered full dress. Long before the bugle tells them to form in line they are ready and hungry.

This ends the morning. We have been warned to write home to parents, but the study period after dinner is the time appointed for that. After a bountiful dinner we see them prepared to write. The big boy will write willingly to some of his folks and loves to write to the girls. He does not have to be reminded that Wednesday and Sunday are letter writing days. The middle sized chap needs a little urging, but the little bear is the one who forgets. He may be so homesick that you dare hardly speak to him on that subject, yet he has to be forced to write regularly.

There are exceptions, of course. Take little Jimsey, for instance, whom I found crying. The minute I looked at him I knew right away what kind of malady he was afflicted with. Says I to him: "Jimsey, old boy, have you written home to your family yet?" "No," he answered, "I don't know how to spell all the words right. You see, I have never been away from home before and never had to write letters to my mother." "Oh, if that's all that ails you, I am the boss letter writer. So, come along with me, young man, and you can dictate and I will write." "Can I do that?" he wanted to know. "Of course you can. The Director will say it is all right." And this is what Jimsey wrote to his mother, at least he dictated and I wrote it:

"Dear Mother, Darling:

"We are here, and I am happy, but so homesick to see you. Do you feel homesick to see me? Let me know. I never thought the world was such a big, lonely place. Is it because you are not with me to hold my hand? I am going to be brave and bite my under lip, and as Biddy says 'Keep a stiff upper lip.' She says half the real truly battles in life have been won by folks keeping up their courage. I don't want to come home, but, mother, if you are passing this way, won't you stop in for a little while?"

"By that time I shall be cured of this complaint. Biddy says its called himevay. It makes you feel weepy all the time, and when night comes and the lights are out that is the time you feel it the worst. Mother, dear, don't pet little brother too much, because he will miss it like I do when he comes to Camp. I know he is only a little boy now, but if you had stopped petting me when I was three months old I should have got used to it by now and not miss you so much.

"If I was not so lonely I could tell you about this lovely place, but I have such a lot to tell you of how I feel. Biddy says I might just as well make this a purely personal letter and get the whole thing out of my system. That, she said, would leave me the rest of the season to describe the other things.

"When the lights are out and from my cot bed I look out of the tent I can see the sky. The moon is way up high, and lots of little stars are shining. Is it the same moon you can see from your window? I hope it is, because you can wish to see me when you look up and I will wish to see you. Then there are so many funny noises. The water seems to be creeping up the shore a little way, then falls back again. What makes it do that, mother? Then some little baby birds keep calling for their mother bird, 'Peep, peep, peep,' just like that. Are they cold, do you think, or are they afraid of falling out of the tree?

"Then all sorts of funny little insects keep flying through the tents. Two or three have little lights in their stomachs, because I saw them. They came and crawled over my netting and the light went out, then in again. Wouldn't it be lovely if we could light our own way like that?

"Give father a great, big hug and tell him his big boy is trying to be a man. Kiss little brother for me, and don't hold his hand any more or he will get so used to it. Biddy says if I want to sleep in her room I can, and then I won't be alone. Well, I will try it in the tent to-night, because if you are going to keep a brave front you have got to do it now. Good-bye, mother, darling. I kiss your photo every night. Write soon to your lonely little boy, Jimsey."

CHAPTER VI.

AFTERNOON SPORTS.

After the study period is over the teams go up to the baseball field for a few games. What exciting times they do have! The boys are divided, and for the sake of sport given colors. So instead of New York and Chicago it is the Red and the Blue.

Thus early in the season they are only friendly games. It is only later in the season, when the trophy and cups are to be fought for, that they play with all their heart and soul.

Now it is fun, fast and furious, to see which side is the strongest. Those who are not playing sit around, cheering or jeering as the case may be. It is all good, healthy sport, and again when the bugle blows for swimming they are ready.

What a rush for towels. The water is a little cooler this afternoon than this morning, but when one has exercised so vigorously it seems just right.

Courage comes to the timid. They strike out into deeper water, find that it is friendly to them, and begin to do fancy strokes.

The good swimmers have started a race with other experts. They mean to swim to the island opposite without any stopover, and are watched by an admiring crowd of youngsters.

Care is taken that no boy goes beyond his depth unless he is a good swimmer. Instructors, in boats, constantly patrol the course, watching every move the boys make.

Well do I remember a funny incident that happened to a visitor last summer. He was a grown man, who said he had been swimming in the Bay of Fundy. As a starter he went in where the little shavers go, and, mark you, in about four feet of water, he went down. One of the faculty, who was watching the boys, saw him disappear. He jumped overboard with his cigar still in his mouth, dived under, brought him up, climbed back into his boat, and calmly went on smoking, leaving the Bay of Fundy hero to wade out.

Some of the boys prefer a short swim, then a row; others just spend the entire time on the chutes, sliding down, either head first or feet first, diving, splashing and climbing back to the float, to do it all over again, looking like a lot of Greek gods in their scanty swimming trunks.

How careful one is in the city about covering up the body quickly for fear of taking cold! Out here the greatest pleasure is after the swim to be in the air and let the sun and wind dry and toughen one. No chill, no cold, just a pleasant glow. Any boy who does this day after day cannot take a cold if he tried to all winter. He is immune from the nasty colds that beset one in this changeable climate.

Is it any wonder that the boys love to be in Camp, where they can strip and get close to Nature?

I have often wondered what Heaven is like, and think it must at least have most beautiful rivers, and flowing streams, where one can bathe.

That is my idea of what Paradise ought to be. Of course, there could be a whole lot of things up there that we have wanted so badly on this earth and could not get, yet for me, the blessed privilege of bathing and swimming in waters pure is celestial.

Maybe the Lord in His goodness took a little bit out of Heaven and planted it in the State of Maine. For where will you go, in this country, outside of that State, and find such a harmonious blending of climate, temperature, water, land, sky and sea as we find there?

But while I am rhapsodizing on the beauties of this State, let me not forget that time flies, and again the bugle sounds the call, "All out."

This time the boys are willing to dress quietly, and spend the next hour resting up after the many duties and pleasures of the day.

There is only a short period between the time we leave the water and the call for supper. When the first call sounds every boy jumps up without a second invitation from the faculty to get into line.

The signal is again given. The line turns right about face, marches to the stirring music of fife and drum, keeping time and forming one of the pleasantest sights we have to show to our visitors.

CHAPTER VII.

EVENING GAMES.

After supper sometimes the porch is cleared for a friendly boxing match or wrestling bout. The boys are chosen who in size and strength are pretty well matched.

There is a well-padded mat, and if the wrestlers stand up first they are stripped. The referee reads the rules to them. They are cautioned against any foul or losing their tempers, and then, at the signal, turned loose.

Do they wrestle? Do they tussle? Do they struggle with might and main to put one another down? You try to find out whether they are wrestling according to Graeco-Roman methods or catch-as-catch-can, and decide it must be a mixture of both. After a spirited round time is called. Each of them goes to his corner to be fanned in a strictly professional way by his seconds.

After one minute's rest they are at it again hammer and tongs, give and take, like two old-timers, all over the mat, first one, then the other having the advantage. They begin to show signs of being winded, so the referee blows his whistle, and again they repair to their respective corners.

After another minute's rest they stand forth for the final round. In this you see some mighty pretty holds. Were they stronger men probably they would be throwing each other over their shoulders, but, being boys, they can't do that. The last round is declared a draw, and as each won one of the other rounds, there is a happy shaking of hands as they go back to their friends.

The next bout being between larger boys, is more interesting. Here we see two splendid types of young manhood. They stand on the mat measuring each other with their eyes, planning just where to take hold, when the whistle blows to begin.

The referee reads the rules to them, lets them clearly understand that he wants no nonsense. "Go ahead," he says, "play the game fair and never mind who wins."

They take each other's hand, the whistle blows and the fun is on. This is genuine, dyed-in-the-wool sport, this is, and all the boys are yelling their heads off for their favorite.

"Go it, old Socks!" "Give it to him, Chesty!" "Say, what did you let him get away with that for?" These and many more such exclamations are heard on all sides.

How easy it is for one to sit on the fence and criticise the other fellow, to tell him just what to do and how to do it! But what a different proposition it looks like when you try it yourself?

The first round is finished and the boys are sitting back almost as tired as the wrestlers. They are being taken care of by the men appointed for that task. As soon as they are rested, they stand up, for all the world like a pair of young bucks in the springtime, who are eager to lock antlers and so long as they conquer the other fellow, don't care how much damage is done to them.

The second round is called; both boys rush in, each eager to be at the other. This is a most spirited and enjoyable affair. It is first one then the other, until one is dizzy watching them. Such beautiful holds! such daring! such a muscular exhibition, that the boys fairly go wild, and when this bout is declared a draw, one cannot hear himself think for the racket.

The third and last round is got over in short time. One of the chaps, watching his chance, puts the other down and of course when his shoulders touch it is all over.

Now for the boxing! We thought we had tasted the cup of happiness to the last drop when the wrestling was on, but no, we had not. There was the sweetest drop yet to be quaffed, and we quaffed it alright, alright, that merry evening.

As usual, the very smallest boys were picked out for the first bout; light weight gloves strapped on, the mat removed, the youngsters told what they were not to do and then turned loose.

They put up a manly little exhibition and at the end of the first round it was only by a hairbreadth that it wasn't called a draw.

In the second round they went at it a little mite more furiously, and the prize ring rules had to be read to them by the Referee. They themselves did not know whether they were fighting with Queensbury rules or plain Johnson tactics. Just having the time of their lives, it was nip and tuck with them, all around the ring; so much so, that when the whistle blew the round was declared a draw and the little chaps being slightly winded, it was decided to let them off the third round.

The next two to step up for the pleasure of boxing were larger boys.

These were well matched in every respect, both as to size, muscle and grit. We knew they would make good. They were both anxious to please their friends, and apart from that were chums. Could two bosom friends come together and try to get the best of each other? That was the thought uppermost in every one's mind. Well, they did, fought like little men, a square, game fight, each bound to win to show there was no queer business; but there were only two rounds fought. Then as each had won one, the boxing bout was ended, to the satisfaction of audience and performers.

But we have other ways of amusing ourselves beside the two I have just mentioned.

The boys who love chess will find partners to play with, and can sit contented, making one and a half moves during the entire evening, if it so please them to deliberate like that.

The checker fiends can play checkers to their heart's content, jumping his men and crowning a man king without half the fuss the usual crowning of kings calls for.

He just sticks one checker on the top of another checker, when he has got to the top row, looks his opponent in the eye, and says "King," then begins to waltz backward and forward up and down, sweeping all the poor little men he finds in his way into the discard. He seems to forget the time when he was only a little man himself. How like live men that is! While some will be considerate of those they have left behind them in the race for fame and fortune, others will step over them or push them out of their way.

That old time game of dominoes must not be forgotten. How many weary hours it has beguiled away! New games may come and new games will go, when we are tired of them, but our pleasant little oblong friends from blank blank to double six will always find a welcome here.

Then Lotto. Why, I am anything but a spring chicken, yet Lotto was an old game when I was young. What a hurry and flurry to cover with bits of glass the numbers as quickly as they were called, and what a joyful yell when you were out first!

On warm nights the boys sit out of doors on the Campus. Some one starts up a college song and the fun begins. All the old time and all the new songs. Among the voices a young tenor is heard; he leads, all the rest joining in the chorus.

Such a medley of sounds—the boy who can sing and is willing, the boy who can't sing and wants to; never mind, when one is young everything goes; it is only when one grows old that one becomes hypercritical.

The night birds cease their songs, so entranced are they at the human warbling. The only feathered night prowler who will not keep quiet is the owl, who persists in joining in the chorus, his part being a question, Who? Who? and then flying quickly away.

These are all innocent little amusements to while away the time until "quarters" sound.

We have other pleasures of a different nature, but those I will leave for another chapter.

"Another evening gone!" you say. "Why, I have done hardly anything at all, and meant to do so much." It is that way every evening. We plan to do all sorts of things, but what with games, songs, feats of strength, spinning of yarns, the time goes all too quickly.

The instructors walk about telling their charges to get a move on. Everybody goes to his tent to undress quickly, plan for another day's fun and frolic; then the bugler blows "Taps" and once more we wrap our covers around us, lying down to peaceful slumber. "So long, Ned." "So long, Joe." "Good night, fellows."

CHAPTER VIII.

CAMPING TRIPS.

One would imagine that being at Camp was enough for the average boy, but it is not always so. After the first novelty has worn off they want to go around seeing other points of interest. Therefore, the weekly Camping trips are planned for them.

We take one day each week, plan some place for each group of boys, who, in charge of their instructor, go out either for a tramping trip or by boat.

One group, for instance, plan to take boats and provisions, row up stream for several miles, make their camp on some island, cook their meals, rest up, swim, enjoy themselves by exploring the island, returning in time for supper.

The next group plan a walking trip; that is much harder on them than the trip by water. They must carry their own supplies, consisting of all kinds of food, potatoes, bread, meat, eggs, coffee, sugar, milk, matches, paper, fruit, besides a cup for each boy, a frying pan, coffee pot and pail for water.

Here you see the way boys act more than on any other trip. The unselfish chap will cheerfully fill his pockets with raw potatoes, try and roll a can of tomatoes, a pound of butter and half dozen eggs altogether, in his rubber coat; put the matches in his tin cup and stagger away. What does it matter if the can of tomatoes does object to being smeared with the butter or the eggs protest at the undue pressure that is put upon them?

When some one yells at him that a streak of yellow is running down his left leg he retorts with, "I don't care if it is. Lots of fellows have streaks of yellow, but they don't want to show it."

We clean him up, show him how to pack hard substances together, and the advantage of putting frail objects by themselves; also that butter is apt to melt if stored away inside one's blouse. That crowd is started on its way quite happy, although the lazy boy is grumbling at having to carry the coffee-pot and frying-pan, while the little chap is leaving a trail of potatoes behind him.

Then there is the lazy lot who don't care to walk, and don't want to row a boat. What do they want?

They will take their share of grub and go up to the ball field. Mind you, they demand some of everything, particularly the food that is easy of preparation. The one and only idea that seems to percolate through their brains is to get a whole lot of food; to make as little effort as possible; to help themselves; to fuss over everything; to be on the verge of starting a half dozen times, only to come back again with some new demand, just like people who decide to take short trips, they know not where, just to get away.

For the rest of the day you may be sure that whenever you look up towards the baseball field you will see one or another of that special party about to come down to the house for more supplies, or just to see what is going on.

How much happier they would have been, had they gone with the crowd! Nine times out of ten if you let a boy have his way, he is not satisfied in the end, and then is ready to put the blame on the country, the lake, the faculty, the dog, but not himself.

There was another lot of boys who were always under the impression that the stay-at-homes were going to have so much better time, so much better food, something better than the rest of the crowd, the sort of chaps that are a little afraid of missing a trick.

Their special stunt was to ask the doctor to look at their ears or throat, complain of an all-gone feeling in the pit of the stomach, a slightly dizzy feeling, toothache or cramps.

When a boy really makes up his mind to stay home there is no limit to his ingenuity in thinking up some plausible excuse. It would take a Philadelphia lawyer to get the best of him.

The only way to take care of those poor little, sick, helpless chaps is to have the cook prepare the plainest kind of fare for them. Leave them beautifully alone and the day will drag along on leaden wings. Long before the rest of the boys return they will be heartily tired of playing sick, and the next camping trip that is planned will be among the first lot of boys to want to go on a long jaunt.

There is heaps of fun in cooking your own dinner. What does it matter if the chicken is scorched on the outside while raw in the middle? The potatoes with crisp skins but underdone in the centre? Corn just warmed through? Coffee hot if muddy? Paper plates? Butter mixed with pepper? Salt mixed with sugar? Water and milk blending beautifully together? Bread and pie in close embrace? Pickles and jam exchanging flavors? As one good little boy said: "What did it matter? Even if you separated them ever so carefully, they were bound to mix up in your stomach; so if they were mixed up beforehand it saved time and trouble afterwards."

You couldn't serve such a meal as the above indoors. It wouldn't taste right, and it would not look right. It needs the open air, with a background of green forest; a gentle breeze blowing the smoke in one's eyes as you watch the fish frying; the cool water at your feet inviting you to jump in, to cool your fevered brow and wash some of the smudge off yourself at the same time. To say nothing of a crowd of hungry boys who have left their manners and fussy notions at home! Here they can get along without a waiter standing at the back of their chair, without an anxious mother coaxing them to eat the tenderloin, so long as they can see their full share coming to them, they are happy.

I know lots of boys who at home are waited upon hand and foot. Yet these same congenial spirits can work like Trojans when out for a day's sport, can build dandy fireplaces with no better material than sand wet with water and bound with cobble stones.

The same boys can cook a meal fit for a king. I don't mean the King of the Cannibal Islands, but a real ruler, because from what I have read the cannibals are not so very particular. Anything that comes their way, so long as it will make a large, juicy meal, will do. They don't care whether the meal is composed of a real good, young missionary or an old tough trader. They would even take a party of elderly spinsters and cook them for quite a while, adding some extra seasoning.

But these boys I have in mind can cook fish, chicken, potatoes and coffee in a way to make you thankful you are living, both before and after the meal.

After the meal is over the question of washing up comes before the board. Most boys would prefer to throw the whole business in the lake, but, having pledged ourselves to see that they were returned promptly to the kitchen, we cannot allow that.

As usual, there are always one or two who are more willing than the rest. They start in to scrape the debris together, put water on the fire to get hot, and in many ways show that there was lost to mankind a good girl when that boy was created.

No matter where one travels, Nature is charming in her virgin freshness. Then look at the difference as soon as human beings step in. The ground is torn up, the flowers trampled underfoot, trees chopped down, empty cans left lying around, on every side upset, and untidiness! Wouldn't it be nice if we just tried to leave the woods and shore as nearly like we found it, not an eyesore, but a pleasure to go back to again?

CHAPTER IX.

ODDS AND ENDS, INCLUDING PRAYERS.

When the days begin to grow hotter and longer most people plan to leave the City. Whether they go to the seashore or to the mountains, to the lake district or some quiet village, they carefully (or so it seems to me) put away their religion along with their winter clothes.

You will find people who are regular attendants at their respective churches all winter long staying away from church, Sunday after Sunday, throughout the summer.

It makes not the slightest difference whether Jew or Gentile, Catholic or Scientist, they all stay away more or less during the summer, and even at Camp, when the call to prayers is sounded, they come in a half-hearted way.

Can one really get along for months without religion? Have they soaked up, absorbed, into their systems enough during the cold weather to tide them over the warm? Can the average church-goer, no matter what church he goes to, store away in his heart and brain enough religion to last, or must he keep on returning to the Fountainhead to be renewed and refreshed?

As I said, the boys straggled in to listen to a true man of God, but some of them came because they had promised to do so, a few just because they really wanted to be there, and the rest because it is human nature to follow a leader.

What excuses we always have ready on hand to show why we have not gone to the House of God! It is too hot, it is too cold, it is dusty, it is wet, no clothes fit to wear, the Sunday dinner to cook, too lazy to get up, all these and a lot more, just because the House of God stands with doors wide open!

You can walk in without the trouble of going to the ticket office for a reserved seat. You don't have to stand in line, glad to buy a standing-room-only ticket. If you desire music, it is there in its purest form for you to listen to. Do you care for singing? Then there you can hear anthems, hymns and oratorios as they never are sung anywhere else.

It needs the sacred silence of the House of God, the subdued coloring, the general air of peace and holiness to bring these things fully to your heart, yet you have to be coaxed to go there.

The House of God has always seemed to me like the house of a very dear friend. Of course, being so far away, we don't think we must pay our respects in person to the Lord. If we have a dear friend (even though full of faults) we keep in touch with him, call upon him, let him know in many ways that we are his very dear friend. Then why not go to the House of God for the same purpose, with the same kind feeling in our heart?

Then the boys sat in silence while the man of God prayed for them, for the good of their souls, that they might grow up doing at all times, whether in company or alone, the right thing in the sight of the Lord, blessed them, sent them on their way, with purer thoughts to help them out of the many pitfalls that beset the feet of youth.

After services are ended we allow the boys to play games. Of what use would it be to compel them to sit quiet all day reading books that they did not care for? Besides, a forced religion isn't worth powder to blow it up.

Let us hope that when fall comes and they take their religion (they have so gently packed away in camphor) out it will not show any signs of decay, no moths or other evidences of dissolution, but a bright, loving light to lead their footsteps to His Throne.

Sunday at Camp is much like any other day, excepting that the laundry is given out and the outgoing wash collected.

The boys form into line under the direction of the faculty, are sent down in companies of ten according to their numbers, to the laundry room, where they receive the clean wash, consisting of personal clothes, besides sheets, towels and pillow slips, take them up to their tents, put them in their trunks, excepting what they put into immediate use.

After breakfast they gather up all the soiled wash, make out a duplicate list, and have them ready when the man calls at each tent for them. Quite a clever system that works out all right.

Sunday afternoon is spent on the water or some game is started up. The usual swimming is indulged in, and by supper time everybody is ready to peck a bit of food, even if they have dined later and had a most bountiful repast.

In the evening the fun begins. Generally on Sunday the Literary Society has an open meeting. Everything goes, from a banjo solo to an imitation fight between two noted prize-fighters.

The little boys recite, the big ones give monologues, our celebrated orchestra renders stirring selections, and the entire Camp joins in the chorus.

The instructors cheerfully help out. It matters not what you ask them to do! Sing a solo? Why, yes; he will be delighted. Sing a duet? Pleased to oblige such an appreciative audience. Join in a quartette? Why, nothing would give him greater happiness.

It makes no difference how silly they have to act. They just go ahead. Anything to please the boys and keep them in good spirits.

Were Hammerstein ever to come out to Camp on a Sunday evening he would find more real talent on our little stage than he has at his own vaudeville house.

The evening ends very happily, all voting it a bully good show. They give three cheers for the performers, and with a final cheer for good measure, "Quarters" are sounded.

It is a happy crowd that slowly wends its way to the tents, and many a laugh is heard as they go over the evening's performance.

The faculty clear the place, leaving everything in apple-pie order for the morrow. "Taps" are sounded by the bugler and another happy day is done.

As we grow older it may take more to please us, but I feel confident that some of these days will be remembered long after we have grown up. Life would, indeed, be for many of us a very sad thing if we had not childhood's happy days to look back on.

CHAPTER X.

FOOTBALL.

Why there should be such excitement about a game of football I have never been able to find out. When all is said and done you can hardly see the players. They are bunched together most of the time. They stand bent over, looking for all the world as though they were about to play leapfrog.

Then some under-sized little shrimp of a fellow begins to yell 4-11-44, 7-28-7-11, and all manner of numbers; he grows fearfully excited over the stupidity of his team; they evidently don't understand the signals.

In a perfect frenzy of passion and despair he raises his voice and almost weeps. Sometimes he says things that are not in the polite letter writer; not the things that a gentle youth would send in a letter to his best girl, but the rest of the team don't seem to mind it at all. The other side is doing the same. They have also a man whose special mission in life seems to be howling with all his might while madly springing up and down.

Again they form and await the whistle of the umpire. Every man acts as though the eyes of the entire sporting world were upon him.

Gee! If they can only get the start; what they won't do to the other side! The whistle blows, one yard gained after a terrific struggle; form again, more numbers yelled in a voice hoarse from much shouting, then they are off again! A splendid kick causing the ball to form a perfect curve as it sails through the air, one great big chap fairly springs up several feet to catch it as it comes down; he runs, and his side, when the whistle blows, have gained five yards. I stand idly watching them, wishing that the game was more familiar to me. It must be a good game, after all is said and done, or people would not go wild about it.

The first half is over. Now the umpire is quite a busy man. Let us trust he has taken out a traveling life insurance policy, for he certainly needs it as he wanders up and down. Each side is filing its protests. If he is to believe them they have each been guilty of everything but piracy on the high seas.

Several boys have been knocked out for a minute. They are being attended to by the surgeon and staff—a liberal sprinkling of water besides massage sets them up again quite eager to join the fray.

The coach calls his crowd around him, scolds some, praises others, warns all to go carefully. The little chap, whose special mission in life seems to be to cuss and yell numbers as fast as he can get them out, is on hand; watches his opportunity to remind them that when he says 8-7-6-5-4 he does not mean 93-2-15; begs them, for sweet love's sake, to go in and win.

The referee blows the whistle. Both sides form. They toss up for the first choice, and off they go.

In spite of one's desire to sit quietly and let them chew each other up like a pack of Kilkenny cats, until nothing but the tails are left, you find yourself yelling, jumping, running along with the rest of the crowd.

"A goal! a goal!" they shriek, and all because one boy has thrown the ball over. Phew! what excitement! what joy for the winners! sympathy for the losers! a happy blending of praise and blame!

No matter where you go it is just as bad; that is, in any English-speaking country.

This fall I saw, while in Lincoln, England, a tremendous crowd coming out of the railroad station. They were pushing and jostling each other. Some were packed six deep in cabs, riding in butchers' carts, on bicycles, on tricycles. I had almost said icicles, because they were going any way so long as they got there. My curiosity at last got the best of me, and I stopped a good-natured looking man. "My friend," I said, "what are you all in such a hurry for? Is there a hanging going on, or has England declared herself a Republic?"

He looked at me with a pitiful smile, as though to pity my ignorance.

"No, Madam," he said, "it is a game of football, and they kick off at 2.30," and off he ran.

On this particular day the Reds won, to the everlasting sorrow of the Blues.

Boys are nice chaps, anyhow. Just as soon as the game is over there is not one bit of hard feeling between victor and vanquished. They shake hands, say better luck next time and are ready for the next game.

If we could carry that spirit with us out into the world, what a lot of good it would do us, as well as the other poor soul who has lost in the game of life. At least let us try and give the other chap a fair show, a run for his money, so to say. Then if we do come out ahead it won't matter so much. A kind word, a loving thought, means a lot to the chap who has lost, while to us it affords some satisfaction to have won modestly, not to fly on the top of the fence, flap our wings and crow like the victorious cock.

CHAPTER XI.

BOATING.

Boating has always been a much-sought-after pastime. The boat, even as little children, we were very fond of was one called Noah's Ark. Ours was filled with cute little animals, and trees, and houses, that gave us great pleasure to arrange, always taking care to make them walk two by two, each couple of bears or elephants or cats, or any other animal, never on any account to put a rat with a cat or a tiger with a goat, as we were taught that they had to pair off the right way.

Noah's ark was a good old boat. From what I can make out it must have been somewhat like a present-day houseboat, while the lower half was like a cattle carrier.

Jolly time Friend Noah must have had to preserve order. Of course, the fear of being thrown overboard probably kept them behaving fairly well. Still it must have been a dreary time for all, not like the boating at Camp.

The Vikings with their war vessels manned by dozens of slaves, some of them below decks where they had to sit chained together, plying the long sweeps for dear life—death for them if they failed—death for them at the end always. Poor, poor fellows! I never read about them but my heart aches.

What thousands of human beings have been sacrificed to bring our civilization up to its present humane standard! That was another kind of boating for you.

We can go on and on, down to the present time, and find in every period something to interest, to shock, to awaken our truest sympathy for those who have gone before, but as this is not a history of boats and boatmen, just an account of our outings, I will not digress any longer.

In the beginning of the season we don't care what kind of a boat we go out in so long as it is a boat, but in a few days we begin to notice the great difference between a flat-bottomed boat and a dory, between a canoe-shaped boat and one with bow and stern. The advantages of each and every one are quickly mastered, until at the end of the first week we have pinned our faith to one particular kind, to the exclusion of all others. Then our usual selfishness begins to show. We charter that boat, and woe be to the fellow who takes it.

A boat that you are used to is like a friend. You seem to get right in mood with it, can tell to a second when to humor it, and in return the boat answers to every move you make. If you like a boat and have been out in it, no matter whether the wind comes up suddenly or a storm threatens, you feel perfectly safe. You can take one oar, stand up at one end and make her go like an obedient steed, ride the waves, turn any way you wish, fool around as long as you like, then make a home run up to the dock with flying colors.

You can do that with a canoe-shaped boat, because, if you are turned around by the current, all you have to do is to turn yourself, and either end of the boat is the stern, as you wish. But so much for a rowboat.

Have you ever tried going out in one of those dinky little sailboats? That is Simon-pure sport for you. When the boat is loaded with her living freight she is probably about six inches above the water line. Any little sudden gust causes her to keel 'way over. Between the jolly captain trying to get the benefit of every puff of wind and the nervous passengers you have the time of your life. All other boating fades away compared to being in a sailboat with just enough breeze to send her along while causing her to keel over at the slightest move. You lie on your stomach on the bottom, letting any bilge water slopping around loose soak into your chest. Of course, you have a swimming suit on. That is advisable, in case you went overboard or the boat turned turtle, a custom our little boat showed a tendency to do on the slightest provocation.

She wasn't the kind of boat that you would have wanted to take a nervous mother out in or any one, in fact, that was not well able to swim; but with congenial companions, who could take care of themselves, there was more fun to be got out of that little boat than any in Camp.

Then there were the motor boats; just made for the rapid consumption of oil. Their motto was: "Maximum of oil with minimum of speed," made out of deference to the Standard Oil Company. No man not extremely wealthy could afford to own one of them. Between drinking oil by the gallon and quarrelling with their igniter they were in dry dock for repairs most of the season.

The real pets of the Camp were the four-oared barges. You felt yourself some boatman when you went out in one of them. With a nifty coxswain in the stern to keep time for you, plenty of room to make your stroke, one of the best fellows as stroke oar, there was not a pleasanter sensation going than to go for a good, long row.

Sometimes you caught a crab, that caused some little delay, while you were spoken to in a real fatherly way by the coxswain. Then again you persisted in making your time to suit yourself without any regard to orders. On one side the oars pulled a much stronger stroke than the other side, constantly skewing the boat, in spite of the best efforts of our tiller ropes. About the only time you showed any kind of form was on the homestretch. Then, playing to the gallery, you put your best efforts into every move of your body, going by the Camp to the landing stage in a manner to make even the Oxford and Cambridge crews look up and take notice.

All that was only practice. The real thing that counted was when the races were planned. Then the boys began to work, to get up early in the morning for special coaching trips, to train in every way, to leave off all sweets; and when a boy does that, you may know he is in dead earnest, until as the day drew near all they could talk, think, eat and sleep was boat talk.

It is a bad thing to wager on a boat race. Yet what a fascination there is in boosting your own side up. You feel sure they will win. Haven't you with heart, soul and mind urged them on for weeks? How can they lose?

You get out and cheer them along, ready to fight with tongue or fists for the glory of your colors. You know it is against Camp rules to wager; yet in the excitement of the moment you promise to forgive debts if you lose and in every way show your faith in your side.

They are ready to start. With many a cheery word for them you wish them Godspeed, at the same time feeling a perfect hatred, for the time being, for your opponents. Gee! if you could only go along with them to cheer them on the course!

They have started, rowing easily to the starting point. Oh! will they never get there? And yet you have warned them about taking it easy to the starting mark. At last they are there, are turning round; the pistol is fired and they are off. "Come on, come on!" you yell, long before they can hear you. They seem to be working with might and main, but what is that? The other team seems to be getting ahead. No; it cannot be. It should not be. In your wild excitement you fall off the rock you are standing on, pulling into the water a couple of onlookers with you. What does a wetting amount to, anyway?

You dare not look when you get back on the rock again, yet, like some horrible monster that fascinates you, you turn around, to see your beloved Blues a boat's length behind. If praying would help them, they can know that you prayed; if weeping for them would have been of any use to save the day, you had done that, too; what was left but the deepest despair.

The Reds won, and my whole nature felt steeped in the deepest blue.

The villain came up to me to claim his wager, with a grin all over his face, making you think of a huge Cheshire cat.

So ended the boat race I had set my heart upon.

> "But what is the use of repining,
> Where there's a will there's a way;
> To-morrow our team may be winning,
> Although your team beat us to-day." —Old Ballad.

CHAPTER XII.

FINAL CONTESTS—TRACK WORK.

After training for weeks one begins to look for some satisfactory results. It is about this time that the boys who have made a special study of track work, under the guidance of a clever instructor, can begin to feel enough confidence in his work to warrant his entering for the final contests.

Oftentimes the boy with the shortest legs has the keenest desire to enter for the standing broad jump. Is it his fault if his legs have not kept pace with his will and brain? You really feel the truest sympathy for him because he always falls an inch or two short. Again he tries, but no go. How can he help it? His spirit is willing, but his legs too short.

The big boy with legs so long that he looks like an animated compass as he strides along is the next to try.

Now you have pinned your faith to him. If he, with those legs, cannot go in and wrest the honors, then who can? He makes a brave enough start, but jumps so wildly that he falls, scattering the dirt all over without gaining enough inches to speak of.

Next to step forward is a spare-built medium sized boy, about the frying size, with not one ounce of flesh to spare, fine bones, slim little ankles, broad chest, good eye for measurement and plenty of strength to carry him over. His followers have great belief in him and frankly tell him they depend upon his work to gain their side so many extra points.

Sometimes if we endow a man with all kinds of virtues, he will really try and live up to them, if only to show us that he can make good. Again he will make good because he wants to do so, both for his own sake and ours. This boy was of that type, loved to do the best in his power to oblige his friends and also because it pleased himself.

He made good, as we all knew he would, winning for his side far more points than they deserved.

The excitement grew so that it was necessary to appoint deputy sheriffs to keep the peace.

All morning were the running, jumping, hurdle races, short sprints, long sprints, broad jumps, standing high, hop skip and jump, every jump known to mankind and a lot that are not known.

The only jump that I did not see done was the one we all are very familiar with, viz., "Jumping to a conclusion," and the reason that was not practised was that there was no prize offered for it.

The next event on the schedule was junior running races. All of the little fellows who had ambition enough, combined with wind and muscle, were entered. It is one thing to think you can run a race, but quite another thing to keep on going after the first excitement is over.

All you can think of as you run, run, run, is the beating of your heart, your breath growing shorter, a sharp pain running through the calves of your legs, a nasty stitch in your side, and then the worst and hardest sound of all, the breathing of the fellow behind you. You feel without looking back that he is gaining on you at every yard.

"If you can only keep going," is your unspoken prayer, until you are around the next turn. "Go it, old boy," you hear them yell. You don't know whether it is intended for you or for the man behind you. Anyway it spurs you on. Why shouldn't you take that yell for encouragement for you? As you turn into the home stretch, the boys who are friendly to you run alongside on the infield cheering and pacing you right up to the wire. Oh! thank goodness, you have broken right through the line, to fall, happy though exhausted, into the arms of your friends.

One race after another is run off during the morning. It matters not whether it is a junior, intermediate or senior race; the same rules and regulations hold good, fair play, no crowding and handicaps where needed. Then at the signal every man to do the best he can, win if possible, never quit unless taken ill, run the race through, even though it is a losing one for you.

In every race there can only be one winner, several who are placed, and the rest are grouped under one head and called "also rans."

Whether it is horses or men the same spirit prevails. The horse with grit will go ahead. Sometimes his shoes don't fit. His bridle is not properly adjusted, hurting his poor mouth fearfully and causing it to bleed. His harness is loose where it ought to be tight. Tight where it ought to be loose. The driver is far more of a brute than the beast he is driving, and yet you will see, in spite of all these drawbacks, that horse, with so much grit, such a game sport, that he will come in winning by a nose, though afterwards one can see him being led to his stable with drooping head and limping feet.

The same with a boy. If he has the pluck, grit, gameness, call it what you like, he will go ahead in spite of all obstacles; win if possible, come second if that is the best he can do, and if he lose, why, then he will look the world in the face knowing he has done his level best.

Separate Games.

Throwing the discus is another manly sport that calls for splendid muscular action, accurate balancing, steady nerves, good eyes and quick action.

This game, old as the hills, is still very popular. Its followers try to play it in both a scientific and artistic manner, taking poses that remind us of Greek gods. There is keen competition between the contestants, and prizes are awarded the winners.

Putting the Shot.

This game might have been handed down from the time of David, who so cleverly put his shot that Goliath was killed, to the surprise and joy of his enemies. Like throwing the discus, it calls for strength, speed and courage. It is a particularly good exercise for the arm and shoulder muscles, but being rather strenuous, is a game for the older boys, who enjoy it very much. Like all other games at Camp, prizes are awarded for the best record.

Quoits.

Still another of the good old games that is as popular on sea as on land. The only difference is that the rings are made of rope for sea use while of iron for those on shore.

On board ship it looks quite easy to throw the ring over the stick, but what with the motion of the vessel and poor calculation, it more often rolls to one side than makes a ringer.

On shore it is not so easy, either. The ground, from being pounded so often by the iron quoits, becomes powdery, the stake is harder to find as the player finds out. One ringer, out of a dozen throws, would be called very fine playing.

It is lots of sport; good to train the eye for measuring distances, the arms to curb their strength, just as the least little bit too much muscle sends the quoits 'way off, and last, teaches one to have infinite patience.

Shuffle Board.

Like quoits, we play this game at Camp as well as at sea. Compare our dandy big table at Camp with firm floor to stand on with the deck of a ship. You cannot begin to make the scores at sea that you can on land. With the best of intentions you send your board along, thinking it will send your opponents off while giving you an added score. Does it do that for you? Well, not always. Most of the time yours goes off or stays on the wrong square, deducting your score while adding to theirs.

On our table at Camp the chances are better for both sides. We play many a spirited game for fun during the season. When the final contests take place this indoor game, as well as any other one, has its turn. Sides are chosen, the losers dropping out while the winners play each other. When the contestants get down to two men the final game is played. As usual, the winner receives a prize.

For the smaller fry the games of checkers, dominoes, etc., etc., offer a chance to even the littlest Camper to compete and win a prize.

Most of the boys would engage in these pastimes for fun, even if there was not any reward offered, but the promise of some prize always stirs up the indolent and timid boy.

CHAPTER XIII.

VISITORS.

After the boys are settled at Camp for a few weeks they begin to look forward to a visit from some of their folks. They plan what they are going to do and what points of interest they will take them to, and hope with all their heart, soul and mind that a large box of good things may be sent up for the tent.

What does it matter if they are forbidden to receive such articles? Either by begging, pleading or some other excuse they let the Director know that this is their first offence. They will only eat a little at a time, and divide it with a lot of boys, thus lessening the danger of overeating, and getting the credit of being generous at one and the same time.

Some parents take long trips themselves while their children are with us. Other parents plan to come as a surprise.

When they drive or auto in the first feeling that most mothers have is amazement at the undressed condition of their offspring. As quickly as they can get out of carriage or automobile they hasten to button up the shirt, if the boy has one on, or to plead with him to put one on if his is off. They feel the breezes blow and shiver at the thought of the boys sleeping in such open tents; advise that the tent flaps be tightly closed at night for fear of the boys taking cold.

They seem to think we are a hardened, cruel crowd because we laugh at their fears. It is not one bit of use trying to convince mother because she won't be convinced. So we save our breath for father. Here we have some ground upon which to sow our seed. We invite him to stay a day or two; "Peel off," we tell him, and "be a boy again. Go in swimming. Go out in a boat. Try a game of ball. Play a set of tennis. Do a little sprint around the running track. We can offer you a lot more sports if you will stay and visit us," we tell him.

In the evenings we can play shuffle board, have some good music, some singing that will make the cats on the back fence green with envy; then last, but not least, we can have a camp-fire. Have you ever been out in the country and helped build a real camp-fire?

After supper every one is pressed into service to help gather the wood. Little chaps stagger along under heavier loads than they can carry, dropping two pieces for every one they pick up, but never saying die. I just love those little gritty kids.

The bigger boys and instructors carry regular old trees, reminding one of an army of ants struggling along manfully to move their quarters.

One or two capable men, who have the art of building bonfires down to a fine point, stay on the field to receive the wood, pile it up and start the fire going.

That is the preliminary only. Are we going to have a corn roast? Then the juicy ears of corn, two for every boy, are brought up to the field. Plenty of good butter and salt in a large bowl is at hand. The boys, visitors and all, form in line, march past the table, where the supplies are heaped up, receive their portion, and hurry along.

By this time the fire has died down to a bright red glow. The smoke and blazes have stopped, the embers being just right to cook the corn; it is stripped of its silk, then the leaves are carefully put back in place and laid down where it will cook through without burning.

Song, laughter and sport pass the time until a fragrant smell assures us that something is doing. Gee whiz! Strip the leaves off. Butter it generously. Never mind if the butter does run down your arm. Close your eyes and sink your teeth into it.

In polite homes they have corn holders, and dainty little knives for splitting it open so that the butter can soak in, and all manner of helps to make corn eating a dainty pleasure. They can have them in their homes all they like, but out here, under this beautiful sky, dotted with stars like tiny lanterns to show us what to do, give me my ear of sweet corn and let me eat it this way.

Sometimes we have a marshmallow roast, generally a treat from one of our kind visitors, who may not have even stayed to enjoy it with us.

After our fire is just right we serve out the marshmallows to the boys. This time they have a very sharp-pointed stick, on which they gently fasten one at a time, holding them close enough to the fire to roast them. They say they are delicious, and, judging from the fact that frequently they eat between them all, about 2,000 marshmallows, they must be very palatable. Personally, I cannot vouch for them, as, somehow or other, I don't like them, either cooked or raw, though my friends persist in treating me to them.

Another treat is a clambake and watermelon feast. That we have on the shore. When packed in sea weed, all manner of good things are roasted, including the faces and hands of the good-natured helpers.

Sweet potatoes roasted this way are delicious, and chicken has an entirely different taste than that cooked in the oven. There is something for every kind of taste and appetite, and plenty to go around.

The modest boy is helped to his share, the independent chap is allowed to help himself, while the greedy fellow is held back for fear he will overload and capsize. At last even the boy who is hard to please declares he has had enough. So with a rousing cheer for the kind visitor whose guests we have been, the bugler sounds "Quarters," a welcome sound to us all. Sometimes the visitor asks if he can become a Camper for a few days or a week. He will gladly pay for the great privilege, for such it is, to be a boy again among boys.

It is granted to him; not one extra for him, mind you. He must take what the

Campers have, the same fare, the same tents, the same beds. If he wishes to join us on these conditions, well and good. Then he can come in and welcome.

From a responsible man of business in the city, in one short night he turns Time back in his flight and becomes again a merry, happy boy, a boy with a capacity for enjoying the simple pleasures of Camp life more than any growing boy can understand.

Hasn't he seen both sides of the picture? Doesn't he know that the plain, clean way of living we have out there is the only true way to exist? What kind of food can give him the satisfaction that this rough fare does? When, with appetite sharpened by sleeping in the open air, enough physical exercise to make his blood flow with renewed purity through his system, he sits at table, he not idly wonders whether there will be anything worth eating, but only hopes there will be two helpings of everything. Like poor, little Oliver Twist, he asks for more.

Such a Visitor will turn to and help the little chaps, will go down to the beach with them, show them how to wash and take care of their clothes, go in the water with them, and take them out in the boats. He acts for all the world like a big, good-hearted brother.

In return there isn't a Camper, from the Director down to the dog, that doesn't adore him, and will at every and any time do anything in his power to make his stay enjoyable.

Our keenest regret is when the day comes for him to leave us. Not alone does he carry back to the city renewed health, strength and spirits, but the happiness of knowing that while he was taking a vacation for himself he was endearing himself to every one at Camp.

Of course, every visitor is not an angel in disguise. We could not expect that. Some come; keep to themselves, and depart, without having caused one ripple on our surface. Yet we are glad to see them, to do all we can for their comfort, and then to wish them Godspeed at their going.

A few come who are ripe with suggestions for the better way to run our affairs. If it makes them happier to suggest, let them go ahead. It won't hurt us any. When one is sure they are doing the right thing it matters little what other people think. We keep on doing the right.

CHAPTER XIV.

LAST DAYS.

To some of the boys last days at Camp bring sadness. They are the ones who, having neither brother nor sister, begin to realize how lonely it will be at home compared to the bustle out here. They love their parents, are anxious to see them, glad to get back to their orderly bedroom and to the daintily set table. All that kind of thing is good to look forward to, yet how lonesome it will be. Of course, they will meet at school and at each other's homes, but not be together all day and night like this.

They plan to be at each other's houses as often as possible; to never, never forget each other, and be sure to share the same tent next season.

All the season long the untidy boy has opened his trunk, reached around any old way for anything he might need at that particular moment, found it, slammed the lid down without regard to hinges or lock. Day after day he has done this, never once looking at his list so carefully pasted on the inside of the cover.

Anyway, what would be the use of looking at the list; it will be time when he packs up to go home. Day after day you pick up quantities of clothing belonging to boys who have thrown them around, remind them that they will be short when they compare their list and stock on hand. They don't care, and very often are saucy. So the time passes away until a couple of days before Camp breaks up.

Now is the time for vain regrets. Where is that bathing towel that they left lying around loose for weeks? What has become of those swimming trunks? Who has seen the mates of both these sneakers? These and fifty more questions are asked of every one in sight.

Sometimes you find some of your belongings under the tent, some in the bathhouse, one or two in the dark room used to keep out the light. Several articles without labels you claim as your own, anything, everything, to help fill that trunk.

Some articles cannot be put in, owing to wear and tear, especially tear. They have gone into the discard long ago. Then, again, some have been borrowed and never returned. The average Camper does not think that "he who goes a-borrowing 'goes a-sorrowing," and cheerfully asks for what he wants, letting the lender do the sorrowing at the end of the season.

The careful boy can pack his trunk, find almost all his clothes and bats, balls, Kodaks, etc., etc., can even close his trunk without the aid of the locksmith. There are more tidy than untidy boys, for which may we be truly thankful.

Along about the time everybody is packing up the boys, who have brought along or bought while in Camp a felt hat, want to have all their friends write their names on it. Some of them are works of art, and one feels quite proud to put his name on, to be in company with so many celebrated signatures.

Often have I wondered what they do with them when they get home. Suppose they hang them up on the walls of their bedrooms as trophies.

After you have written on his hat, very often you write in some book for him. About half the Camp is writing on each other's hats, pants or books. Everywhere you go you will see boys armed with pens, making you think of the old saying about the pen being mightier than the sword.

A general resting up for everybody is advocated after the final contests. That gives one a chance to relax and rest up before going home.

Lessons are stopped; the hour being devoted to siesta instead.

Boys who have all the season neglected their letter-writing tasks begin to get very busy. You will be besieged by requests for paper, envelopes and stamps. They intend letting the family know they are coming.

The boy who during the entire season has sent a blank piece of paper in his envelope, by that means assuring them that no news is good news, now undertakes to write a real letter to apprise them of his return. This so frightens the family that they send a despatch asking if all's well.

The little boys are all very anxious to be met at the depot, also to remind the folks to have a good breakfast ready.

Home-coming always seems sweeter if there is some one to meet us, but we cannot all have loving fathers, devoted mothers, affectionate aunts, sisters or cousins. So the boy who has no one to meet him is not left all alone, but is personally seen to his home or train, as the case may be.

Music and song, games and jollity pass the time every evening until a few nights before the end. Then our celebrated artists give a show.

Whatever we should do without some of our friends I cannot say. What cheerful spirits they bring to bear! How willing they are to do any and every thing, from painting the scenery to painting their own faces!

We can call upon them at any time for help, tell them "You must be a villain, a hero, a lover, a drummer." No matter what we ask for, some of them are ready and willing.

The show cannot fail, the critics who sit in front, and who are more to be dreaded than Alan Dale or Acton Davis, only spur us on to do the best that is in us. We have rehearsed over and over again until those who haven't clean forgot every word are letter perfect.

Sometimes the villain will make a better hero. All right, we give him that role. Again the heroine would look better as the father. That is easily managed. Change clothes and you change sex at the same time.

Nothing daunts us. We would not enjoy the show half so much if all were smooth sailing.

The night arrives at last to give it; you really would not think these were all city boys, who were used to everything from grand opera to vaudeville. So eager are they to help, to advise, to get the best seats, that tremendous excitement prevails all over Camp.

It is rather hard to dress a group of actors and actresses when your principal stock in trade consists of two rolls of crepe paper, some puffs of artificial hair and a few ribbons. Makes one think of "a rag and a bone and a hank of hair."

We have the rags and the hank of hair, and the boys furnish the bones. We manage with the aid of tinfoil, crepe paper and odds and ends of our personal wardrobe to make quite a decent showing.

The show goes off without any hitch. Everybody is good-natured; the critics assure us it was very good, and we clean up the mess, very happy to have been of service once more.

With a vote of thanks to all the willing workers who helped us, the boys once more are glad to obey the bugler when he sounds "Quarters."

They undress quickly, not at all minding going to bed with faces covered with grease, paint or charcoal. Youth does not bother about its complexion. By morning most of it is on the pillow slip, and soap and water will clean up the rest.

The theatrical effects are all carefully packed away, to do duty for another season. The lamps are put out, the curtain rolled up, scenery stored and finis written on the season's offerings.

Lots of work. Lots of worry. Little to do with. Plenty of people to please, and yet! What pleasure in pleasing others! How happy if only they were satisfied! Could I have my choice, in all sincerity, give me the chance to please the children and I could die happy.

The bugler is blowing "Taps." The lights are going out. Once more a sweet good-night to you.

CHAPTER XV.

AWARDING PRIZES.

Every season it is just the same. As the last night draws near there is great excitement among all the boys. Those who have earned medals, cups or prizes try to appear unconcerned, while the rest of the Campers handle, fondle and criticise the gifts.

We ourselves, who expect none, and wouldn't know what to do with a medal if one was given to us, are just as eager and joyful as the smallest Camper there.

When all is ready, what a hush! You can actually hear yourself think as the Director stands up. He looks around with happy smile at the roomful of waiting boys. Begins to read from a list in his hand the name of some one fortunate fellow, who steps forward to receive his medal or cup, as the case may be. Everybody must see it, read the inscription, look at the engraving, look at the case to hold it, before returning it to the winner and owner.

It is the same with each and every boy, whether the medal is of gold, silver or bronze, whether he received it for swimming or rowing, for running or jumping, for feats of strength, like putting the shot or throwing the discus. What matter if it was for football or baseball, tennis or diving? It is a medal, given for merit, and as such appreciated by both winner and friends.

The most popular boy is awarded. The best all-around Camper is medalled. There is hardly an act of courage or endurance that is passed by without some recognition. Such an uproar as greets each new hero!

While we enjoy it with them ever so much, yet we are glad when at last they are all awarded, leaving us the pleasure of hearing the different members of the faculty called upon. The bashful man hardly gets a chance. He is guyed until he sits down. Indeed, there seems to be an understanding between all the boys not to allow any of the faculty to speak. It is one huge laugh from start to finish.

Time after time another man is called upon to rise and express his opinions, or, if he wishes, thank the boys for being so good to him during the season. It's no go. He might just as well sit down and save his breath to cool his porridge.

The rest of the evening is given up to yelling, shouting, singing and having a generally jolly time.

Boys who are very wise have taken the precaution to lock all their belongings up. Fear of burglars? No! A general rough house is looked for on this last night. For fun they will dump each other's trunks or beds.

No one's property is sacred. You can carefully lock your door, but if there is a crevice large enough to let a spider in they will crawl through that, turn your room upside down, not leaving one article in its place, then crawl out again, leaving both door and window locked. How could they have gotten in? No one can tell.

We have serious thoughts of bidding for a turret from some battleship and using that as a room. Nothing lighter would be of any use. It is long after the usual hour for "Taps" to sound, and we wonder why. The bugler is there, but no bugle is to be found. Some boy has hidden it. So on this, our last night in Camp we have to depend upon the instructors, who collect their boys, march them to their tents and stay there, keeping them company while they undress.

Most of them are really too tired to try any games on the other tents, and without any of the trouble we had anticipated they are very soon ready for the signal. As "Taps" cannot be blown the whistle in the hands of the Director is made to take its place.

One shrill blast and the lights go out. "Good-night fellows, lots of fun going home to-morrow."

CHAPTER XVI.

LEAVING CAMP.

Bright and early they are all up and dressed, only as anxious to be off as they were to get here the beginning of the season.

Long before there is any possibility of the wagons coming for them they stand, looking up the road, like sister Anne in the story of Bluebeard.

Some of them are really ready. Most of them are not. It is always at the last moment that one finds most important articles that ought to have been snugly stowed away in the bottom of the trunks, lying under the bed.

One boy is stuffing all his soiled clothes in his rubber boots. Not such a bad idea. You cannot make rubber boots go into a tiny little place, so may as well fill them up.

Another is tearing everything out of his trunk to repack it, having found that there is no room on top for his blankets. Still another solves his problem by throwing away everything he thinks he won't need for the winter. Whether that suits his parents as well as it does him history sayeth not.

How the average mother is able to put such quantities of clothes and shoes and sporting goods in that same trunk before it left home and have room to spare has always been a mystery to him. Maybe if the mothers were to let the boy himself do his packing, while they looked on, it would teach the boy a good practical lesson, and at the end of the season prevent many a heartache.

By the time breakfast is over the wagons begin to arrive. Those who are ready make a wild dash for the best-looking rig. "But not so quick, my friend. You may as well climb out and wait for your instructors, who are going along with you. No need of crowding. There is plenty of room for all."

Are they really so anxious to be off, or is it just the last bit of Camp frolic? At the same time, from previous experience, my advice is to take it easy up to a certain point. On this, our last day in Camp don't let us neglect one thing that we ought to do for the good of the Camp, and yet while we are putting everything in place, locking up all the articles that ought to be locked, at the same time you help half a hundred boys to get their belongings together.

Tie one of the little boy's shoe laces, lend another one a collar button, give a safety pin to another, find a lost hat for a third, put a bandage on a fourth, close up bags, open trunks, strap suit cases, fetch, carry and help anywhere, any one, anybody. Of course, you are going to do all this. In your inmost heart you hope you will be able to take one farewell swim, and still have time to dress like a civilized being, but nothing is certain here.

Just as you decide to put the drugs away and empty the bottles out so they won't freeze during the winter, one of the boys comes into the hospital to have a cut dressed. "How on the face of the earth did you do that? And on the last day, too. Pity you could not remember to cut yourself during office hours." His excuse is that he found his pocket knife that he thought he had lost, in his other pants. Was so glad to see it that he just opened it to see if it would cut. It did.

We wash the wound, tie it up and shoo him out. Are we ever going to get away?

We had always divided the season into three periods, calling them as they affected us, Mad, Glad and Sad.

Mad the first part, until everything got into working order. Glad the second part, because things were going along all right, and Sad the last part, because we hated to leave.

But to-day we have reversed it, and the Sad is first; the Mad is last.

As I said a little while ago, my advice up to a certain point is to take it easy, but in order to do so you had better carefully follow this recipe:

Take one horse, one wagon, one set of harness and one whip. You can, if you wish, separate them, or, if you have room, leave them together. Watch your opportunity and hide them deep in the woods, where they can keep cool and quiet. When you are ready to use them step very carefully up to the horse, grasp the bridle and, jumping into the wagon, with the whip in your hand, drive off.

You might invite one or two of your friends to go along, but be sure to leave a seat for yourself.

We have often heard of people sprinting for a wager, and we have been an eye-witness of people who sprinted for a train, because they stayed back too long. Therefore, by following the above famous recipe, you will find it digestible and not hard to prepare.

Now, having left Camp at last, we have another most beautiful ride through shady roads, where the foliage is turning all colors, where Nature with a most lavish paint brush is tinting the maples, turning the apples into balls of gold and red, causing the golden rod to look like a golden border alongside the road. What a riot of color! Wild astors, gentian, foxgloves, everlasting flowers shading from yellow to darkest brown!

Summer still here, but autumn creeping in a little further each day!

Every minute of that drive is pleasure. We laugh. We sing. We joke with each other. What good friends we have all become! And yet how sad to think that in a few short hours we may part, perhaps never to meet again. Is it any wonder that I, who have had many partings, should feel sad? Is life only to be made up of partings? Or are we to look forward to happy meetings?

Who knows? Anyway, nothing is to be gained by spoiling our last few hours together. So again let us be merry and bright, adopting for our motto, "Sufficient unto the day is the evil thereof."

The farmers come to the doors of the farm-houses to bid us good-bye and Godspeed. The same motherly cows stand looking at us with their serious eyes. The same frisky calves run along on the inside of the fence, a little older, a little wiser, but still recognizing kindred spirits among us, as when we travelled this road a few short weeks ago.

How quickly the time has flown! It is only impetuous youth who desires the time to fly. In later years he dreads to see it pass so quickly. If it is a long lane that never has a turning, then ours has been quite a long one. At last we come in sight of the depot.

What a merry crowd! It is quite an event to see us come and go, almost as good as the circus, but much cheaper.

Any of the Campers who have any change left are busily trying to get rid of it. They don't mean to be caught with any money on them when they get home if they can help it. The druggist, the fruit store, the candy shop, all get their share, and when the train pulls in, the boys can happily state that they have only car fare left.

The ride on the train affords plenty of enjoyment to old and young. The passengers who are not Campers are very much amused at the antics of those that are.

When they were going to Camp, they spent the hours before they got there by saying all they were going to do; now on leaving, they entertain each other by retailing all the fun they have had while there.

We get back to Portland in plenty of time for supper.

Everything looks clean, dainty and appetizing. The boys tuck in as though they never knew when they were going to get another square feed.

At last Nature, good old soul that she is, cried, "Stop or take the consequences," and most of them did. One or two who thought they had room for just a little more stowed away enough to give them a nice little stomach-ache, which ought to have taught them better.

After supper we went aboard the train, and settled ourselves comfortably until it was time to start.

Our berths were assigned to us and, as on our outward trip, the little shavers were put together at one end of the car in charge of instructors and Biddy.

Soon after we were all aboard, the train drew out of the station. For some little time, boys visited one another in the different cars. Then the long-lost bugle was discovered. The bugler was summoned and ordered to blow "Quarters." Every man Jack of them at once obeyed, found out where he was to sleep and in less than one hour, when Taps were sounded, all were in bed.

For the last time the bugler stood in turn in every car sounding Taps, the porter ready to put the lights out. In that narrow space it sounded very loud, very clear and most beautiful.

"Good night, fellows; see you in the morning. Don't forget to come up to the house to-morrow night."

"Here, you, stop taking all the bed clothes." "Oh, you chaps in that upper berth, don't throw cracker crumbs around."

"Please, sir, can we have the window opened?" "Please, sir, can we have the window closed?" Laughter, happiness and teasing until the last one is asleep!

Throughout the long night nothing is heard but the click of the rails as the train drives on, the brakeman passing through with his green and red lanterns, the faithful instructors seeing that all are covered, our beloved Director himself looking out for the welfare of his flock.

Biddy herself in her favorite corner. But like an old mother hen who has carefully brought up the families of several other hens, now that her chickens are able to scratch for themselves, and when nightfall comes have wings strong enough to fly to the top of the roost, she feels she can stretch her legs, then one wing, then the other, cramped by long hovering, and with a sigh of complete satisfaction close her eyes in sleep, secure in the thought that "He who slumbers not nor sleeps" will watch and protect her flock.

We still have to get dressed on the train, and that is something to look forward to.

Before daylight some of the boys are up and about. It is of no use trying to sleep any more, so we may as well tidy ourselves up, wash our faces, if there is any water, brush each other off, and try and look just a bit tidy when we get to the station.

Parents and friends will be so happy to see us that they will forgive us, no matter how wild and woolly we look.

To see such a company of tanned and healthy boys is well worth coming to the depot and waiting for belated trains.

As we hand over the last boy to his folks, what a lot of satisfaction it affords us to know and feel we have played the game fair, and given every one a square deal!

Once more we hear the Camp calls, sounding strange here in the city. Good byes are exchanged, thanks expressed, hopes for another season, and at last they have all been taken away from us.

We can go our way in peace, tracing, with happy finger, the word that ends our season's labor.

(FINIS)

Lector House believes that a society develops through a two-fold approach of continuous learning and adaptation, which is derived from the study of classic literary works spread across the historic timeline of literature records. Therefore, we aim at reviving, repairing and redeveloping all those inaccessible or damaged but historically as well as culturally important literature across subjects so that the future generations may have an opportunity to study and learn from past works to embark upon a journey of creating a better future.

This book is a result of an effort made by Lector House towards making a contribution to the preservation and repair of original ancient works which might hold historical significance to the approach of continuous learning across subjects.

HAPPY READING & LEARNING!

LECTOR HOUSE

LECTOR HOUSE LLP

E-MAIL: info@lectorhouse.com

9 789356 145979

Printed by Libri Plureos GmbH in Hamburg,
Germany

9 789356 145979